Fez 1495R-WN

HOME
STYLE
BY
CITY

Ideas and Inspiration from Paris, London, New York,
Los Angeles, and Copenhagen

Text, photography, concept, illustrations, and design
Ida Magntorn

CHRONICLE BOOKS
SAN FRANCISCO

Contents

Flea Market Directory

Paris

Marché aux Puces de Saint-Ouen, between Saint-Ouen and Clignancourt, 18th arrondissement, open Saturday, Sunday, and Monday

Marché aux Puces de la Porte de Vanves, Avenue Georges Lafenestre, Rue Marc Sangnier, 14th arrondissement, open Saturday and Sunday

Vide greniers (attic/garden flea markets): http://vide-greniers.org

London

Portobello Road Market, Notting Hill, open Saturday

Camden Market, Camden High Street, Buck Street, open all days

Brick Lane, Shoreditch High Street, open Sunday

Carboots (flea markets on wheels): www.carbootjunction.com

New York

Hell's Kitchen Flea Market, West 39th Street between 9th and 10th Avenues, open Saturday and Sunday

West 25th Street Flea, Broadway at 6th Avenue, open Saturday and Sunday

The Antiques Garage, 112 West 25th Street, open Saturday and Sunday

Brooklyn Flea, 50 Kent Avenue, between N. 11th and N. 12th Streets, Williamsburg, open Sunday

Los Angeles

Long Beach Antique Market, 4901 E. Conant Street, Long Beach, open the third Sunday each month

Melrose Trading Post, Fairfax High School, 7850 Melrose Avenue, open Sunday

Santa Monica Flea Market, Airport Avenue and S. Bundy Drive, Santa Monica, open the first and fourth Sunday each month

The Rose Bowl Flea Market, 1001 Rose Bowl Drive, Pasadena, open the second Sunday each month

Copenhagen

Ravnsborggade, Nørrebro, 200 Copenhagen, open four Sundays a year

Market near Trinitats Kirken (Trinity Church) and Rundetårn, Kobmagergade 52A, open Wednesdays May through October

Antiques stores open all year, check for open hours

Foreword

The sun is hot, and half of the family got tired a long time ago, but my travel partner and I are not giving up just yet. We have to touch the silky, airy fabrics. Try on sunglasses, fiddle with jewelry, and examine every ornate coffee mug.

This is the way we spend our vacations most often. The more I explore flea markets overseas, the more I become fascinated by the differences and likenesses between cultures. I see the commonalities—who sells skeleton parts and old clock faces as precious treasures; in what cities I can find odd doll heads, stuffed squirrels, or porcelain dogs.

The flea markets and what I find there, along with what's bought and sold, reflect the ambience of the homes in that location, as well as the lifestyle of the city. How do the flea market finds resemble a genuine New York loft or a Parisian attic apartment with its wrought-iron balcony? What kind of vintage items are the city's inhabitants drawn to, and how do they use their flea market finds? Most often, I wonder how the purchased objects look in somebody's home: How are they styled? Where are they placed?

I traveled around my five favorite cities, I researched, I questioned, I took pictures.

My goal was to find homes that captured the city—nothing too exclusive, but ones that felt homey and real. I was fortunate enough to sit at many kitchen tables and have inspiring conversations about community, vintage objects, interior design secrets, and the art of decorating with the right things in the right places.

Posing on Jessica Barensfeld and Simon Howell's rooftop in Williamsburg, Brooklyn.

Relaxing at Tracy Wilkinson's home in Eagle Rock, Los Angeles.

The Revelation

In this book you will follow me to the tiniest nooks and crannies of my vintage-loving friends' homes in Paris, London, New York, Los Angeles, and Copenhagen.

The pages are packed with tricks and tips I learned from them, and I'll show how to create the same feeling in your home.

Decorating is about telling a story in order to create an ambience. Think about the mood you want to evoke in your home. Think of forgotten things and far-flung destinations. Let your imagination fly!

Each city features a flea market checklist with typical finds should you be visiting the area, as well as things you can search for closer to home. You'll also find step-by-step tips on how to get the looks. To offer inspiration for each city's setting, I include lists of books, songs, and movies to help you capture the right mood in your home.

Paris

Paris's soul is
feminine and poetic,
floatingly romantic,
and a bit decadent.

An old Parisian apartment
is perfectly askew, with
a small balcony where
you can enjoy breakfast.
On the table you'll find
simple vases, fading
bouquets, and strewn
rose petals.

Faint tunes of French
accordion music twinkle
through the rooms.
Delicate blouses, handbags,
and lingerie hang on the
walls. The décor feels
unplanned, simple, and
a bit disheveled.

The secret:
Nonchalant elegance.

Paris's Mood

Where does that very special feeling in Paris come from? The answer, among other things, is in the unique light. L'heure bleue is the suggestive hour between the evening and the night, with anticipation in the air. The grand facades glimmer in the light. It almost blinds you in the summer and is like a shimmer over the city the rest of the year.

Character

Thanks to Baron Haussmann, Paris is big and dazzling. Per Napoléon III's request in the middle of the eighteenth century, Haussmann planned wide boulevards through the narrow, medieval neighborhoods. New white structures rose along the grand avenues and hid the smaller buildings. These edifices shine in the front, while the small, narrow residences are hidden in the back.

This formula also applies to Haussmann-era apartments: First, you'll find two lavish living rooms, one after another, separated by paned-glass double doors. Behind the living room is a private area intersected by a hallway to a bathroom and bedroom. A small kitchen has service stairs to the backyard. Not all apartments of the Haussmann era were built in this style, but almost all share these features: tall windows and a French balcony.

Cultural Heritage

Paris's cultural heritage hovers over the city: seventeenth-century Versailles with its gold mirrors and crystal chandeliers; the decadence under the fin de siècle and belle epoque with cancan dancers at the Place Pigalle and Moulin Rouge; the intellectual cafés and smoky bars where deep existential discussions took place; and the ever-present silhouette of the Eiffel Tower.

This rich culture informs how Parisians decorate their homes.

3 *steps for getting in the Paris mood*

✔ Immerse yourself in the French language by watching movies filmed in Paris (see page 32). Feel the environment *à la parisienne* in Camille's bedroom in the film version of *Hunting and Gathering*; take notice of the bedside table and the upholstered chairs.

✔ Listen to "La vie en rose" by Edith Piaf.

✔ Get inspired by famous French women like Catherine Deneuve, Juliette Binoche, and Audrey Tautou, or Jane Birkin and her daughters Charlotte Gainsbourg and Lou Doillon. These beauties represent the classic French woman who would live in the classic French apartment.

Poetic Style

Your way to a Paris-style apartment

*How can you create a feminine and poetic atmosphere?
With a few secrets, of course, and a bit of everyday
sensuality. Add a note of chic nonchalance and a pinch
of decadence.*

Here's how to achieve it.

Bedroom Atmosphere

Start with the foundation of the room, which can be the
bed or the sofa. Be sure it is soft, fluffy, and sensual. Allow
yourself to dive into the romance. Add some French touches
to your space.

✔ An authentic Parisian atmosphere always includes
a French iron bed, but if you don't have one, you can
never go wrong with roses: wilting roses in a vase, a
string of rose-shaped lights on a wall, or big fabric
roses by the bed's headboard.

✔ Lace and embroidered pillows in pastel hues provide
atmosphere without drawing too much attention.
Scour flea markets to find the perfect ones—the older
they are, the better.

✔ A small lamp with a red shade gives just enough
decadent light.

Haute Couture

Paris is home to some of the biggest fashion designers—and this should be reflected in the décor. Use clothing and accessories as eye-catchers: a transparent blouse, a boa, a handbag à la Chanel, or a pair of elegant boots. Some accents to hang on the wall:

✔ Ballet shoes—to guide your thoughts to graceful dancers on big stages. The look is beautiful but also strict and somber, just like the city. It captures the city's vintage romance.

✔ Straw hat with a bow—evoking what the Frenchwoman wears on a hot summer day.

✔ Lingerie—not necessarily with lace, but having the feel of a vintage lingerie boutique.

Casual Chic

In addition to feminine details, soft ambience, and fashion accessories, you need something casual that doesn't appear as considered. For example, create an artfully cluttered desk.

A French desk can contain things like:

✔ Small flowery boxes adorned with knickknacks on top, underneath, and in between.

✔ Black-and-white photographs scattered in a charming disarray.

✔ A desk chair with shabby edges, maybe with velvet upholstery, preferably with small wheels on the front legs.

✔ Sunglasses within reach, hanging on a nail that happened to be left on the wall.

Paris Flea Markets

The block might seem enclosed and secretive, but when you look under the curtain of clinging vines between just the right café and bistro, it's only a few steps down to the serpentine alleys of the flea market at Porte de Clignancourt. A whole cluttered block of vendors. Everything here is exquisitely French and graceful: the rickety birdcages, the worn velvet chairs, the beautiful and expensive paintings.

Brocante

"Brocante, La Madeleine, Samedi" reads the sign on a lamppost. On a Saturday, the day of the flea market, all the streets around the Madeleine church are filled with an array of things. Someone has brought all his mirrors, someone else his entire collection of suitcases. There are wooden stamps, café au lait bowls, and romantic landscape paintings. It ends in just few hours, but our bags are brimming with all kinds of finds, and over my shoulder hangs a crystal chandelier.

Draw inspiration from this list of what French women search for at the flea market.

FLEA MARKET CHECKLIST

1. Ornate birdcages
2. Feminine blouses
3. Old-fashioned typewriters
4. Crocheted lace tablecloths
5. Crackled mirrors
6. Old chandelier crystals
7. Purses, large and small
8. Lingerie
9. Ballet shoes
10. Old dolls and doll heads

Crystal Chandelier

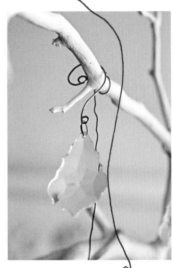

Une vraie parisienne, a true Parisian woman, has a crystal chandelier in her home. If you can't find one at the flea market, you can make it yourself.

GET THE LOOK

1. Gather old, mismatched prisms. You can often buy them inexpensively when they come from broken chandeliers.

2. Find a tree branch and paint it white, in order to give it a drawing-room feel. Hang the branch from the ceiling with a sturdy string.

3. Tape an electric cord to the branch. Wind three lights around the branch and connect them to the cord.

4. Decorate with prisms of different sizes and shapes. Add sparkle with something glittery, such as a mini disco ball.

Parisian Still Life

A curated mix of unusual things is a fundamental feature of a Parisian still life.
Collect objects with different characteristics for the perfect display.

Go with the basic rule: Place bigger objects in the background and smaller ones in the front. Build the base with something large and tall, for example, a Versailles-inspired mirror or a palm tree in a nice pot for an art deco feel. An ornate candleholder is always a great eye-catcher.

Finesse the Look

Keep in mind that the French style is not just a powdery dream. A garland of paper hearts looks best if you pair it with something bolder: a black-and-white picture of a rock star or just a simple old picture frame.

Explore other contrasts. If you like old dolls, then search for doll heads, for a decadent and dark look.

Let the arrangement find its own life. Do not restrict yourself to a table or dresser. Work the tableau up the walls or out to the sides. Think about creating interest using unexpected combinations, like making a simple apple crate into a shelf for knickknacks.

tip

Use a typewriter as a holder for photos. Mix vintage photos with photo booth pictures to create a nice retro feel. Display them in no apparent order.

The French-woman's Secret

The French effortlessness must be captured with subtlety. Here is a typical French trick: let a lacy transparent blouse—a romantic, feminine one—flutter in the window, the hanger appearing as if someone left it there in a hurry, on the way to do something else. Perhaps it is thought through, but it will bring an air of spontaneity.

Raw Poetry

The Frenchwoman puts a little bit of everything into the interior, making it dreamy but at the same time raw and poetic with a touch of darkness. A clock face without hands, an anatomical drawing of Siamese twins. Along with these gloomy touches, something glittery and fun is added: a string of colorful lights or a spinning disco ball.

Continue thinking in new ways. Do you have a door that does not fit in with the rest of the room? You can use it as a message board; create a collage with old newspaper articles and other pictures.

Asymmetry

No need to strive for harmony in your space, though you may add some purposefully organized areas. Try a shelf above or under a busy wall of paintings. To maintain a Parisian air, fill your shelf with French books, all having white spines, but add a pop of color with two bright spines. Coral red or black? Lemon yellow or mustard brown?

Mirror Décor

The Archetype of Parisian Decadence

A crackled mirror is the perfect Parisian touch. Here are some tips for creating a more brittle sensuality.

✔ Leave a rose or lily to wilt in its vase.

✔ Mix small and large mirrors.

✔ Place green plants in the bathroom so that they reflect in the mirror.

✔ Hang a necklace over the edge of the mirror to strengthen the feminine touch.

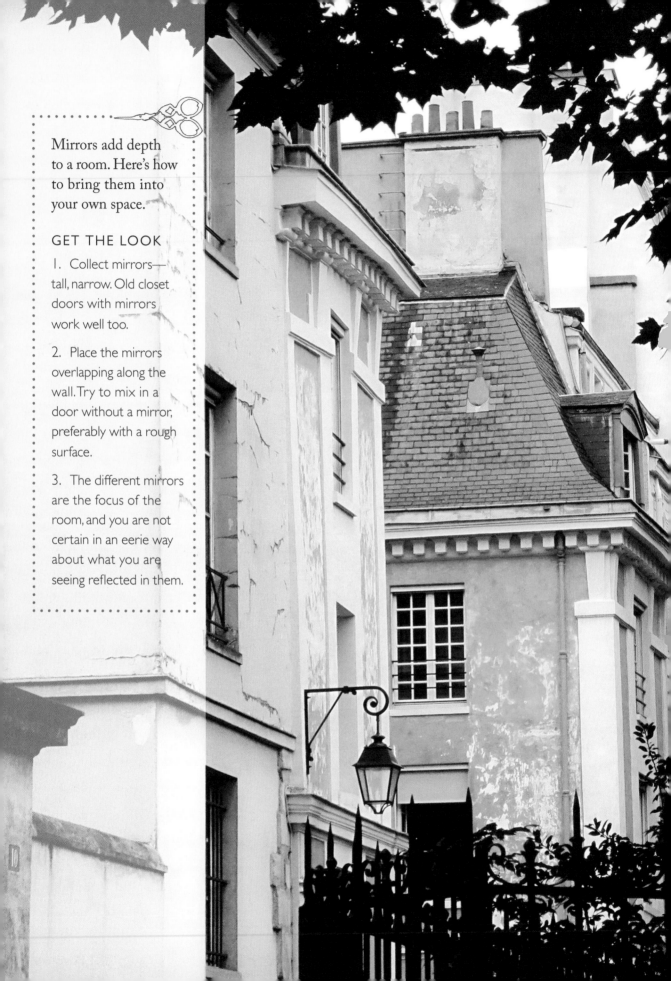

Mirrors add depth to a room. Here's how to bring them into your own space.

GET THE LOOK

1. Collect mirrors—tall, narrow. Old closet doors with mirrors work well too.

2. Place the mirrors overlapping along the wall. Try to mix in a door without a mirror, preferably with a rough surface.

3. The different mirrors are the focus of the room, and you are not certain in an eerie way about what you are seeing reflected in them.

Wall of Mirrors

Lace Décor

A simple yet elegant way to give furniture a Parisian look is to cover it with a fabric that has a simple lace pattern. Drape a round crocheted tablecloth on a chair or cover the whole sofa with a crocheted bedcover.

You can make a ceiling lamp from miniature lace swatches, and it will shed a glimmering light in a room. Creating the lamp may take some patience, so listen to the playlist on page 36 as you make it and you'll get into the right Parisian mood.

"See Paris and die of pleasure."

Guy de Maupassant, 1850–1893

GET THE LOOK

1. Blow up a large balloon and cover it with plastic wrap.

2. Mix some wallpaper glue. Completely soak about five lace cloths in the glue.

3. Cover half of the balloon with the cloths, overlapping them so that they stick together. Let dry for at least 2 days.

4. Complete the rest of the lamp in the same way, using five more cloths. Leave a space at the top, about 2¾ in/7 cm, through which a light socket and bulb will fit. Let the balloon dry for at least another 2 days.

5. Once the balloon is completely dried, poke a hole on the top. Pull out the plastic wrap and the balloon, and insert the bulb.

6. Hang the lamp using fishing line tied to the holes in the lace.

The Color Palette

The colors of
Paris are pale
and powdery.
If you could
touch them, they
would be as
smooth as velvet,
with a feeling
of tea and soap
bubbles, a bit
transparent.

Peach
Apricot
Light lavender
Light red
Powdery pink
Tea
Aged silver
Moonlight yellow
Emerald green
Dove blue

The Kitchen

3 *steps to a French kitchen*

✔ A simple mixture of objects, a little uneven and odd, sets the tone. Use pastel colors like turquoise and sunny yellow to cover up any imperfections.

✔ Dull essentials, like the refrigerator, which does not have a set place in a Parisian apartment, can be hidden in the décor. A black-and-white poster or another detail with character takes the focus away from the refrigerator and gives a tougher look in contrast to the pastel details. (Even if you have a perfectly matching refrigerator and freezer, you can never go wrong with an edgy touch of black and white.)

✔ A basic kitchen trolley with wire baskets adds a pleasantly uneven look, much like a Parisian balcony. Here, the ornate can be found in the baskets on the counter and on the spice shelves.

MOVIES TO WATCH

1. *Moulin Rouge*, Baz Luhrmann

2. *Amélie*, Jean-Pierre Jeunet

3. *Three Colors: Blue*, Krzysztof Kieślowski

4. *The Double Life of Véronique*, Krzysztof Kieślowski

5. *Breathless*, Jean-Luc Godard

tip

Collect plates with nice patterns, preferably roses. Keep them in plain sight for a floral hint. Or stack French café au lait bowls and blue-green glass bottles for more colorful strokes.

Birdcages

Ornate and beautiful birdcages sit nicely on a little table, exuding a Parisian aura. A chirping canary in the corner can set the mood, but if a bird is not desired, then the cage can be used to make a statement in other ways.

❦ An empty cage can be nice in all its simplicity.

❦ Turn the cage into a still life of objects you like: a feather in a vase, a perfume bottle, a porcelain dog.

❦ Make the cage into a chandelier. Put a cord and light socket through the top of the cage and hang it on a chain or sturdy string from the ceiling. Lace a rope of lights through the bars so that the cage glitters.

❦ Decorate the cage with birds or butterflies from a hobby store.

❦ Lace the cage with clinging vines and use it as a trellis with room for a flowerpot.

BOOKS TO READ

1. *The Elegance of the Hedgehog*, Muriel Barbery

2. *Hunting and Gathering*, Anna Gavalda

3. *Kiffe Kiffe Tomorrow*, Faïza Guène

4. *Memoirs of a Dutiful Daughter*, Simone de Beauvoir

5. *Parisian Chic: A Style Guide*, Inès de la Fressange

PLAYLIST

1. "Moi je joue" (Brigitte Bardot, Alain Goraguer)

2. "Sous le ciel de Paris" (Édith Piaf)

3. "Je ne regrette rien" (Édith Piaf)

4. "Comment te dire adieu?" (François Hardy)

5. "Te souviens-tu?" (Jane Birkin, Manu Chao)

6. "Poupée de cire poupée de son" (France Gall)

7. "Jolie Coquine" (Caravan Palace)

8. "La Bohème" (Charles Aznavour)

9. "Quelqu'un m'a dit" (Carla Bruni)

10. "Et moi, et moi, et moi" (Jacques Dutronc)

11. "Bonnie and Clyde" (Brigitte Bardot, Serge Gainsbourg)

12. "La vie en rose" (Édith Piaf)

Au revoir, Paris

London

The soul of London is eccentric, full of exaggeration and humor. A typical townhouse is tall and narrow with a winding staircase. The rooms are dark but glimmer with Victorian gold accents and an extravagance of flowers.

Here lives a storyteller who mixes the attitude of the British punk band the Sex Pistols with a love for queens and *Alice in Wonderland*.

A bit dreamlike, with mismatched proportions and clashes of styles.

The secret:
There are no boundaries.

London's Mood

What creates that buzzing feeling of London? The answer can be found in the swarm of the city. The markets, where cauliflower is crammed next to vintage dresses and old suitcases, with a distant colonial gust of New Delhi. The underground rumbling through the earth. The red double-deckers cruising around like large ships together with the bowler-looking taxicabs.

Character

The tall, narrow townhouses of London are somewhat tilted and almost lean against each other. They were built during different royal eras: Georgian, Victorian, Edwardian. Like the clothing of the time, all were constructed with a love for decoration—lots of stucco in the ceilings. Some are patched and were repaired following the bombings during World War II. Many have pointed roofs, are a bit secluded, and perhaps have a miniature cottage garden in the backyard. These houses are mixed in with a few palaces, worker housing, and workshops. But it's the swarm we want to find.

Cultural Heritage

Rumor has it that Anna Maria Russell, the sixth duchess of Bedford, introduced the afternoon tea. But it was actually Queen Victoria's royal tea party at Buckingham Palace that started the tradition. I like the tea party from *Alice in Wonderland*. The Mad Hatter's infinitely long table with an infinite number of teapots, cookie trays, and cups of different sizes, shapes, and patterns.

Combine the chaos of the Mad Hatter's tea party with Oscar Wilde's signature quip, "The only way to get rid of a temptation is to yield to it," and you have the signature London home. How do you access that signature?

3 *steps for getting in the London mood*

- ✔ Listen to "London Calling" by the Clash.
- ✔ Put on a kettle for tea and sit down with Virginia Woolf to follow Mrs. Dalloway's day in London.
- ✔ Alternate between watching the chaotic comedy *A Fish Called Wanda* and following the looks of British style icons Alexa Chung and Kate Moss.

Eccentric Style

Your way to a London home

Who lives in this home? Someone who loves flowers and gold accents, and who reimagines Victorian heritage in her own way. Someone who mixes Mary Poppins and David Bowie, flowery cretonnes with ottomans in gold, and who uses an old lace tablecloth as a curtain in the kitchen.

Here's how to bring British florals into your home the London way.

✔ Find a basic sofa that makes the flowery print unexpected.
✔ Dare to mix: it's part courage and part practice.
✔ Start with colors of the same shade, for example, blue. Blue shades never clash, and they work well for combining large-flower patterns and Liberty's small-flower style.

tips

- Try to mix different colors from the British palette, for example, moss green and rust, olive green and pink, or cinnamon brown and cherry.

- For a more refined look, match the sofa with the same flower pattern as the curtains. Head to the flea market to gather as much of the same kind of fabric as possible.

Unexpected Combinations

✔ Try mixing orange leather with blue floral textiles on large swiveling chairs from the '60s and '70s.
✔ Pair metallic-green and snakeskin patterns.
✔ Yellow and plaid add the perfect British touch.

Hints of Gold

✔ Look for candleholders in brass; they are inexpensive and shine nicely when flames reflect off them.
✔ Try to find candelabras with roses or cherubs for the walls.
✔ Keep your eye out for objects that match the extravagant empire style of the 1810s. Look for things with Egyptian inspiration: sphinxes, eagles, and palmettes.

1810 versus 1970

Mix empire style with 1970s leather furniture. Think British and *crazy*. What else can you add? Something bright and colorful, such as a blinking crucifix of colored lightbulbs. If you find one big enough, lean it against the wall.

More combinations that complement empire style:
✔ Floor lamp with a colorful shade
✔ Plastic chairs
✔ Large-flower patterns
✔ Everything orange

Other combinations that intensify empire style:
✔ Palm trees in pots
✔ Velvet- and plush-covered chairs
✔ Everything burgundy

To round off the character of the room, add something romantic, like paintings of flowers or idyllic portraits leaning against the wall.

Home Style by City

London Flea Markets

On Portobello Road, all the houses are painted in pastels. Think of Hugh Grant peeking out through the blue door at the bookstore with Julia Roberts in the film *Notting Hill*.

    The sidewalks are filled with vendors' tables carrying my favorite coffee mugs, with Queen Elizabeth on them. Simply shaped, ordinary, and bordering on inconspicuous, these mugs become treasures when emblazoned with the queen's face.

Pop-Up Market

From the charming Notting Hill, we continue to the other side of town, the hip paradise of Brick Lane, filled with people. A secret door with a handwritten sign is ajar: "pop-up market." Two floors down, the place is teeming with knickknacks and fun clothes. The salespeople all look straight out of a 1920s movie, dressed in secondhand suits and accompanying vests. Or in the nicest cream-colored dress made of muslin gauze, with a flower diadem in the hair—enormous and fantastic. Lips painted red. Someone is sitting at an old sewing machine repairing finds from the flea market. A man wearing a turban is selling bunches of peacock feathers. These are all things you might find at the London flea market. Here is what you should look for when you get there.

FLEA MARKET CHECKLIST

1. Lace tablecloths
2. Porcelain dogs
3. Flower-patterned handkerchiefs
4. Old lamp bases
5. Small plates with swirly patterns
6. Floral paintings
7. Mugs with the queen's portrait
8. Everything golden and bombastic: vases, candle-holders, mirrors, flower-patterned curtains
9. Liberty textiles

Sweet Dreams

In a British bedroom, a fireplace is a given. As is a well-stocked library with books stacked up to the ceiling. Walls painted in a subtle hue give the room a natural British feel.

If you don't have a bedroom with a fireplace, a dresser, preferably in a baroque or empire style, will do equally well as a central place in the room to showcase beautiful objects.

✔ Paint the dresser black to evoke the right mood.
✔ Surround it with bookcases that reach the ceiling. Add a ladder to suggest an authentic British library.
✔ A somewhat antique mirror on top of the fireplace or dresser will add depth to the room.
✔ Try to find the most elaborate of vases. The more baroque, the better.
✔ Old perfume bottles are a must.
✔ Add your finest black-and-white photos and drawings. If you have a favorite painting, put it on the wall, or stack a few paintings leaning against the wall.

"He took my jacket and showed me into a living room that made my thoughts go to Oscar Wilde."

From *84, Charing Cross Road* by Helene Hanff

BOOKS TO READ

1. 84, Charing Cross Road, Helene Hanff

2. Saturday, Ian McEwan

3. White Teeth, Zadie Smith

4. Mrs. Dalloway, Virginia Woolf

5. A Christmas Carol, Charles Dickens

6. London Style Guide: Eat Sleep Shop, Saska Graville

MOVIES TO WATCH

1. Notting Hill, Roger Michell

2. Sherlock Holmes, Guy Ritchie

3. Sliding Doors, Peter Howitt

4. The Picture of Dorian Gray, Albert Lewin

5. A Fish Called Wanda, Charles Crichton

tips

The London feel is built on the play of dimensions, surprises, and subtle colors.

✔ A saturated deep blue on the walls creates the mysterious atmosphere of a fairy tale. If you don't want to paint the walls, simply choose blankets and cushions of the same color. A brown lampshade provides a pleasant dampened light.

✔ Look for objects disguised as animals. Lamps in the shape of dogs, preferably life-size or, even better, unnaturally large. Or try a picture on the wall of an oversized animal, such as an eagle, for a somewhat creepy effect.

✔ Let the unexpected peek out. Or take the décor one step further. What can serve as a coffee table? Think of something with the right height. Perhaps a sleigh?

Dimensions

tips

Cozy Kitchen

In a London kitchen, you want to bring out the sense that something unexpected will show up. Camouflage unattractive but needed items. Take the edge off the boring musts with something that surprises.

✔ A dark stuffed bird on the water heater
✔ A whole window covered with tulle and Victorian lace

As a contrast to the lace curtains, use a simple metal storage shelf for your pantry. Add jars, packages, cups, and glasses.

Decorated Plates

Everything is welcome in the London kitchen. A sea horse in a glass frame, an ornate baroque-style bowl to store ladles and spatulas, or beetle decorating plates.

GET THE LOOK

1. Collect odd plates, preferably with gold accents, swirls, and flowers. Make sure they are clean and dry. Wipe them with denatured alcohol.

2. Try to find old dishwasher-proof ceramic decal transfers at the flea market, or use new ones.

3. Wet the decal paper so that the backing sheet comes off easily.

4. Apply the patterns to the porcelain. Make sure to smooth out any bubbles, and let dry.

5. Bake the plates in the oven. Follow the instructions on the package of decals. You need a kiln to make the plates dishwasher proof. Or you can bake them in the kitchen oven and use the plates as décor.

Sea Horses

Painted Lamp

tips

An unexpected lamp base gives a quick and simple British touch to the room. Romantic couples, dancing ballerinas, and rose blossoms; a harlequin statue or a naked lady—the more fantastical, the better. Painting the base a single color makes a bold statement.

GET THE LOOK

1. Wipe the lamp clean, with denatured alcohol if needed.

2. Start by painting a layer of primer so that the paint will adhere better.

3. Apply several thin layers of paint on your lamp base, taking care to get into all recesses. Let dry according to the instructions on the paint can. To avoid brushstrokes and if your base has a lot of curves, consider using spray paint.

Color suggestions:
- Army green is fun, since it's so unexpected.
- Try cerise or neon yellow for a pop.
- Black is refined, and white is stylish.

British Bath

Only in London would you find a bathtub in the bedroom! It's not uncommon to see a washbasin with skinny lathed legs. Here are some ways to decorate the room.

- ✔ Hang up sun hats and straw hats that recall a summer swim, or hang a kimono on a hanger.
- ✔ Choose beautiful mirrors, preferably in a Venetian style.
- ✔ Hang a pearl necklace on the towel hook.

Lace Curtains

Transforming a lace tablecloth with long fringes into a curtain is a simple yet arresting way to let in light.

GET THE LOOK

1. Fold the tablecloth with the front end hanging lower than the back.

2. Attach curtain clamps evenly on the top edge and hang on a curtain rod.

PLAYLIST

1. "London Calling"
(The Clash)

2. "Rock the Casbah"
(The Clash)

3. "The Lovecats"
(The Cure)

4. "Penny Lane"
(The Beatles)

5. "Back to Black"
(Amy Winehouse)

6. "Changes"
(David Bowie)

7. "Running Up That
Hill" (Kate Bush)

8. "This Charming
Man" (The Smiths)

9. "Sgt. Pepper's
Lonely Hearts Club
Band" (The Beatles)

10. "Breezeblocks"
(Alt-J)

11. "The Passenger"
(Siouxsie and the
Banshees)

05/03/2012

The Color Palette

London's colors are racy. Subtle and mysterious with a lot of depth, sometimes gloomy, sometimes neon.

Midnight blue
Velvet blue
Moss green
Olive green
Bottle green
Rust
Cinnamon
Cherry red
Bordeaux
Gold

Party Glitter

The legacy of Queen Victoria in London: everything has a glittery touch.

- ✔ A sequin top on the wall says more than words with its immediate festive spirit. Collect old necklaces and bracelets on the same hanger.
- ✔ Suitcases act as storage while lending a glamorous feel when all-white cases are stacked along a wall.
- ✔ Don't forget a well-decorated bar cart, mandatory in every British home.

New York

New York's soul is artistically intelligent, bohemian, and smart. The classic New York loft is in an old factory building and has open spaces, roughcast walls, and a concrete floor.

Graceful windows framed in cast iron reflect the building's heart. Minor repairs show here and there, and a cool morning light streams into the one soaring room, its ceiling high, high, high above. A bike leans against the wall. Greenery trails down from above. The décor is effortlessly simple, laid-back, never showing off.

The secret:
An unfailing sense of simple style.

Peacock Butterfly 2533R-WN
(*Hamadryas io*)

utterfly 478-MN

New York's Mood

What is it that makes New York's mood so special? Could it be the feeling you get when you crane your neck to see the glittering gold top of the Chrysler Building? Or is it the view from a roof terrace, that skybar, on the sixty-second floor? Or is it the evening sun shimmering across the skyscrapers?

Character

The first skyscraper in the United States was built at the turn of the nineteenth century. Decades later in Manhattan, buildings grew higher than ever before. Skyscrapers and art deco cast-iron confections are New York's architectural expression. The Brooklyn Bridge, of steel cable and stone, with its elegant, fairy-tale street-lamps lighting up at dusk, opened in 1883. The Williamsburg Bridge, finished twenty years later, spans from lower Manhattan to the Williamsburg area of Brooklyn, with parts red-painted and some of it covered with graffiti. Many of the city's characteristic factory lofts are found in Brooklyn. Old industrial buildings with their fine turn-of-the-nineteenth-century details have been converted into apartments and studios, with communal gardens and indoor jungles. That's where we're headed.

½

Peacock Butterfly 2533R-WN
(*Hamadryas io*)

Cultural Heritage

Imagine '20s jazz, with Ella Fitzgerald and Louis Armstrong at the smoke-filled Cotton Club in Harlem. That's the foundation of New York's cultural inheritance. From there, the culture moved through Andy Warhol's Factory, which drew icons like Allen Ginsberg and Bob Dylan, on to Patti Smith and Robert Mapplethorpe, and right to '70s disco glitter at Studio 54. And the ever-present silhouettes of the skyscrapers and the Statue of Liberty. These are the basic ingredients for décor the New York way—always with a touch of rock 'n' roll in your soul.

3 *steps for getting in the New York mood*

✔ Put on your favorite New York song. Try "Sunday Morning" by the Velvet Underground; it perfectly evokes cool morning light filtering through delicate windowpanes.

✔ Get lost in a book set in New York. Imagine yourself in Violet and Bill's apartment on the Lower East Side in Siri Hustvedt's *What I Loved*.

✔ Simple but artistic—that's the vibe we're after in the city that never sleeps.

Loft Style

*Your way to a typical
New York—style apartment*

Whom shall we imagine living here? An artist and ascetic bohemian—what would she or he have left behind? Brushes, feathers, books?

Look around your home with a raw, almost primitive eye. If you have any surfaces that are a touch unfinished, make the most of them by emphasizing details that have an industrial feel. Are there exposed water pipes? Or a concrete wall hiding behind that wallpaper?

After that, it's a matter of softening the hard edges, rounding off the corners. Classic oriental rugs give an inviting feel. Sisal mats are an inexpensive alternative and make a good compromise.

You'll also need a color accent if you're to capture the feel of a classic New York loft. It could be a bright red armchair or a saffron-yellow chaise longue. Now you're nearly there and can begin fine-tuning with details and flea market finds.

Indoor Greenery

Green leaves trailing down from the ceiling, a palm in the corner, a fig tree in a window alcove. The contrast between vivid green and industrial gray is an elegant one. Your own city oasis can be formed by graceful patterns of ferns against a shabby wall, and passionflowers stretching up to meet the sun. When choosing plants, look for ones with a variety of leaf shapes: spider plants, with their arching leaves and hanging runners, or other trailing plants such as string-of-hearts or maidenhair vine. Plants with large foliage also work well to form a backdrop of greenery.

GET THE LOOK

1. Search for an array of hanging baskets. Macramé would be best, but try to find a variety of materials: basketry, wood, ceramics.

2. If your ceiling has exposed pipes, it's easy to hang baskets from them. Otherwise, look to screw in hooks or simply hang baskets from curtain rods. Make sure your baskets hang at different levels—you can use S-hooks to adjust the various heights.

3. Before putting plants in your basket, make sure that the bottom is lined with plastic or another material that will prevent leaks. Next, place a layer of perlite to provide drainage. Pour soil into your basket and pot the plant.

4. Don't let the plants get stranded up near the ceiling. Use shelves and small tables to allow your indoor garden to spread out. With seven or eight plants, the mood is set.

Plant Recipes

Hanging Basket Garden
Care: Somewhat difficult, mostly because it can be tricky to
water so high up, but makes a fantastic statement. Plants to use:
golden pothos, arrowhead plant, spider plant, passionflower, and
Chinese Virginia creeper.

Mediterranean Garden
Care: Needs sun, warmth, and a little water now and then. Plants
to use: fig tree, citrus-scented rose geranium, rubber plant, and chili.

Desert Garden
Care: Minimal, and it tolerates drought, heat, and direct sunlight.
Plants to use: succulents, aloe vera, desert rose, wax plant, and
mother-in-law's tongue.

New York Flea Markets

Waves lap at Brooklyn's shore, and the view of Manhattan across the East River is enchanting. A stone's throw away, the Brooklyn Flea is in full swing. Boxes full of bits of skeletons and squirrel nests jostle with antique clock-faces. You can find gorgeous tin ceiling tiles rescued from demolition sites. Some have been fashioned into wall art or mirrors. They are in good company with jewelry made from typewriter keys and artwork from old maps.

Among Skyscrapers

The ferry from the quay at Kent Avenue goes to Midtown Manhattan. Walk across Midtown, and you come to the Hell's Kitchen Flea Market. Squeezed between the sky-scrapers on 25th Street is another flea market—filled with tailor's dummies, military surplus, and old globes. With the tall buildings looming over the flea market tables, it feels a very long way up to the sky. Farther down 25th is the Antiques Garage. Every floor is filled with bits and bobs: vintage American cameras, paintings, and flower baskets being sold by eccentric old ladies.

That's what flea market Saturday in New York can look like. So, what should you be keeping an eye out for?

FLEA MARKET CHECKLIST

1. Pots and hanging baskets
2. Industrial lamps
3. Skeletons and skulls
4. Butterflies
5. Clockfaces
6. Tin ceiling tiles
7. Beautiful bottles
8. Old flags
9. Feathers and plumes
10. Books

Brownstones

Brownstone houses, typical in areas such as Park Slope in Brooklyn, were built of local sandstone toward the end of the nineteenth century. Often, rooms in these houses have special ceilings of beautifully patterned tin sheets, which were a cheaper alternative to European plaster moldings.

Lamps as Art

With a nail and a little hammering, you can make an industrial piece to complement your New York–style loft.

GET THE LOOK

1. Draw the pattern you want onto a metal lampshade. It could be a zigzag line or small dots that make a flower. Or perhaps a simple phrase like "Good morning."

2. Place a piece of wood under the shade for protection. Hold the shade steady by using a vise, or get someone to hold the shade for you.

3. Carefully punch holes along the marked lines using a thin nail, such as a fishing nail, and a hammer.

4. If you want to give the shade an extra handmade touch, wrap coarse string tightly around the neck of the lamp and all along the wire. Finish off with a small knot near the plug.

Nature's Wonders

Once you've studied enough skeletons, skulls, and bones at flea markets, you'll begin to understand their beauty. Soon, it becomes impossible to turn away from those little jewel-like treasures. The purity and the clean lines fascinate. As décor, they can form a pleasing still life in combination with butterflies and feathers.

Peacock Butterfly   2533R-WN
(*Hamadryas io*)

Seashells have a beauty similar to skeletons—spreading corals, flat scallops, and round half-moon cowries. Explore beaches and comb flea markets for the perfect shells to adorn your mirror. Make sure the shells are as clean as possible so that they adhere to the mirror well.

GET THE LOOK

1. Find a simple mirror and paint the frame white. Allow the paint to dry.

2. Using clear epoxy, glue your treasures on the frame. Start with common scallops and cockles along the outer edge, and fill in with the rarer shells. Allow the glue to dry.

3. When the decorations are secure and fully dried, it's time to start painting. Use a white water-based craft paint, which will work on most materials. Paint two or three coats for an even, smooth result.

Seashell
Mirror

"Jazz is the music of the body."

Anaïs Nin

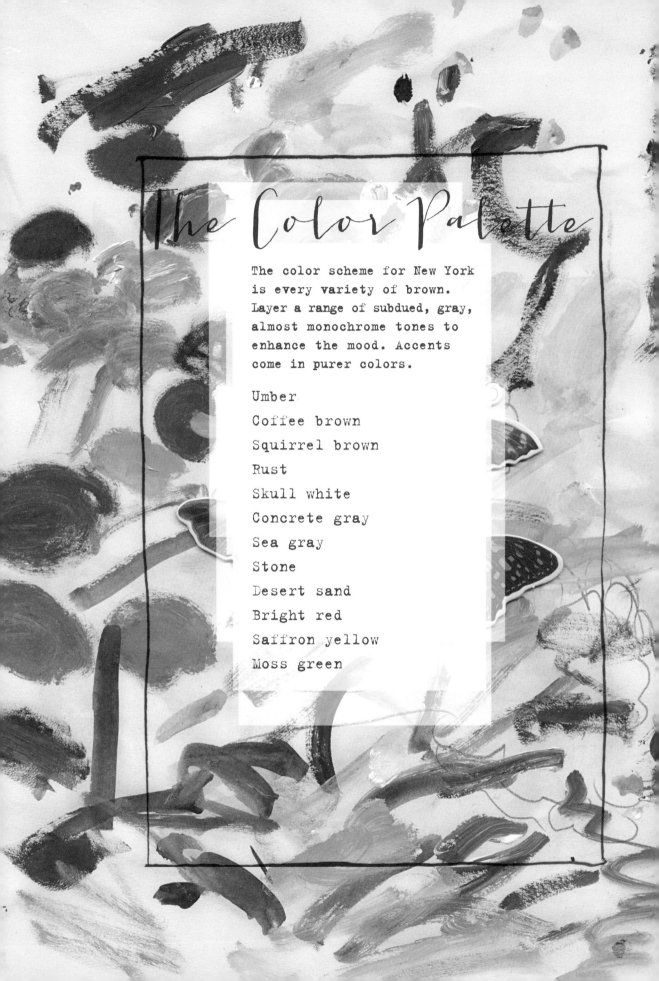

The Color Palette

The color scheme for New York is every variety of brown. Layer a range of subdued, gray, almost monochrome tones to enhance the mood. Accents come in purer colors.

Umber
Coffee brown
Squirrel brown
Rust
Skull white
Concrete gray
Sea gray
Stone
Desert sand
Bright red
Saffron yellow
Moss green

Book Art

A New Yorker never ever throws away a book, instead pasing it on to a bookshop or an antiques shop. Sometimes, though, books are too precious to pass on, and so one must find new ways to make use of them. Here are two clever ideas for repurposing surplus books the New York way, direct from Brooklyn.

GET THE LOOK: BOOK TABLE

1. Start with a desk that has thin round legs. You'll need a drill bit that is slightly larger than the diameter of your table legs. Collect enough books for four table legs. The exact number will vary depending on the thickness of the books and the height of the table. A mix of medium-thick paperbacks and hardbacks works best.

2. Drill carefully through one book at a time. Make sure that the book does not fall apart; this is a lot easier if it's not too thick.

3. Turn the table upside down. Slide the books onto the table leg.

4. After adding the last book on each leg, put a cross of tape over the hole so that the books don't fall off when you turn the table upright. Use thick gaffer's tape or something similar.

5. Turn the table upright. Adjust the books so that they form a slightly disordered stack up each leg of the table.

GET THE LOOK: BOOKSHELVES

1. Carefully remove all the pages of the book so that only the cover remains.

2. Cut a suitable piece of plywood to size—it should be about 1 in/ 2.5 cm smaller than the book cover on all sides. Glue the plywood between the covers with wood glue. Allow to dry.

3. Carefully drilling through the cover and the plywood, make two holes, one on each edge.

4. Screw angle brackets into the holes. Mount the shelf on the wall.

Stars and Stripes

The flag on the wall has forty-three stars, which means it dates from before 1890. This flag is said to have been found rolled up under the beams in the attic of an abandoned house.

Bottled Greenery

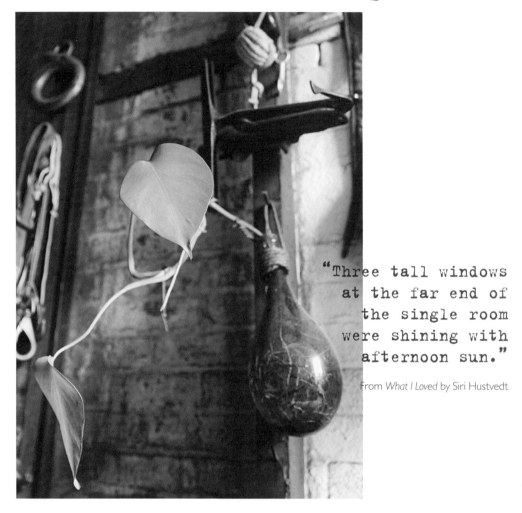

"Three tall windows
at the far end of
the single room
were shining with
afternoon sun."

From *What I Loved* by Siri Hustvedt

Small green details will lend cohesiveness to the plants all around
your space. Look for pretty tinted bottles that will hide water residue.

GET THE LOOK

1. Take a cutting from your favorite plant, and place it in the bottle.

2. Pour in enough water to cover a good portion of the stem.
Add more water now and then as needed, and soon roots will
appear. Don't water too much, or the roots will rot.

3. Tie decorative knots in coarse twine or rope to hang the bottle.

PLAYLIST

1. "Cigarettes and Chocolate Milk" (Rufus Wainwright)

2. "Tom's Diner" (Suzanne Vega)

3. "New York, I Love You But You're Bringing Me Down" (LCD Soundsystem)

4. "Walk on the Wild Side" (Lou Reed)

5. "Sunday Morning" (The Velvet Underground)

6. "The 59th Street Bridge Song" (Simon and Garfunkel)

7. "New York, New York" (Frank Sinatra)

8. "Don't Think Twice, It's All Right" (Bob Dylan)

9. "Sitting on Top of the World" (Lenny Kravitz)

10. "First We Take Manhattan" (Leonard Cohen)

BOOKS TO READ

1. *What I Loved*, Siri Hustvedt

2. *The History of Love*, Nicole Krauss

3. *The New York Trilogy*, Paul Auster

4. *OK, amen*, Nina Solomin

5. *Just Kids*, Patti Smith

Bike as Décor

True New Yorkers take their bicycles up to their lofts and put them to use as part of the design so they never feel in the way.

MOVIES TO WATCH

1. Annie Hall, Woody Allen

2. Green Card, Peter Weir

3. New York Stories, Martin Scorsese, Woody Allen, and Francis Ford Coppola

4. Taxi Driver, Martin Scorsese

5. The Godfather, Francis Ford Coppola

Los Angeles

L.A.'s soul is soaked
in sunshine. It's bohemian,
warm, and soft, with a true
hippie living in its heart.
A Californian bungalow
keeps the doors open to
the sun, and the border
between inside and outside
is as thin as the horizon.
Desert, mountains, or ocean
are always nearby.

On the porch hangs
a hammock for napping.
A surfboard leans against
the wall. In the windows
hang sun-bleached
curtains. Above the bed
is a dream catcher,
emitting calm and a sense
of weightlessness.

The secret:
Ethnic blends.

The L.A. Mood

What is it that creates that feel of the City of Angels? The palm trees that sway up above, the sun that heats, and the low houses that make the sky seem so close. The blend of soft and hard, the unexpected proximity of the roar of the big city, and a love of nature. Places filled with spirituality, and at its heart, the feeling that anything is possible.

Character

The residential streets are lined with palm trees and bungalows, or so-called craftsman houses of a 1920s style. These houses are inspired by the arts and crafts movement and have pointed roofs, Swiss chalet–style decorations, and dark wood finishes, and almost all have a porch to take a nap on.

In other places, the houses are influenced by the Case Study House style of Charles and Ray Eames's home from the late 1940s, in wood, glass, and steel.

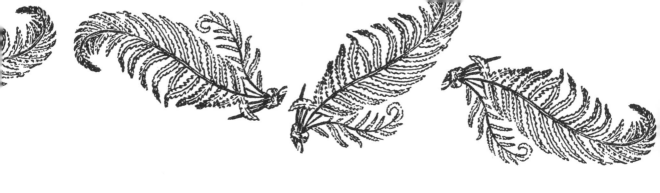

Cultural Heritage

The Hollywood Walk of Fame, celebrities, the Oscars gala—Hollywood and the movie industry have dominated the cultural scene since the 1920s. Charlie Chaplin's silent movies, musicals like *Singin' in the Rain*, the noir movies of the 1940s, and the film *Pulp Fiction* of the mid-1990s are inspired by Los Angeles. And all around, the famous Hollywood sign is visible.

This culture mixes easily with the 1960s love generation and the musicians of Laurel Canyon, as well as the surf and skate culture of Venice Beach.

Together, these elements make up the foundation of Los Angeles.

3 *steps for getting in the California state of mind*

- ✔ Put on the Beach Boys' "Surfin' USA" or the Mamas and the Papas' "California Dreamin'."
- ✔ Watch a bit of Baz Luhrmann's *Romeo + Juliet*, shot in Venice Beach. Think of summer, palm trees, and flowers dangling in your hair.
- ✔ Add some touches of local craftsmanship to your home.

Bungalow Style

Your way to a typical L.A.-style room

Who might live in our Californian home? A cosmopolitan jet-setter who draws inspiration from every corner of the world and creates a simple mix of Bedouin style and Native American and jungle-inspired elements.

tip

Fill a chest with beautiful rocks and good karma.

Bedouin Style

Focus on fabrics and draperies to easily create the atmosphere of a tentlike den. An already existing alcove is an extra bonus, but not required. Just decide which part of the room is good to shield off.

- ✔ Put two curtain rods one above the other. This will allow you to overlap the drapes. Fasten curtain rings with clamps so you can easily change the textiles.
- ✔ Mix fabrics; use at least four different ones to get a layered effect. Different patterns on the front and back give a sense of depth when the curtains flutter.
- ✔ Put overlapping rugs of various sizes on the floor. Try to find rugs in soft sandy colors.

The Den

The drapes should feel a bit as if you're inside a child's fort. Subtle and soft colors enhance the contrast with the bright room outside. It should feel like getting a warm hug.

- ✔ Put small lamps in the corners to create cozy lighting.
- ✔ Paint the walls a dark mauve, and choose a lighter hue, maybe lavender, for the ceiling.
- ✔ Use crates as shelves. This works in any room, but will be best in a cramped den with a slanted ceiling. Stack excess books around the shelf to let the bookcase extend.

tip

Paint the ceiling in stripes using soft colors like off-white and light yellow. The stripes will give the feel of a circus big top.

Home Style by City

L. A. Flea Markets

You spot hippie dresses in tie-dyed patterns and long shell necklaces. The guy at the end of the tent is loudly announcing that all the contents of a Beverly Hills house are for sale. Objects are priced by the square foot. Things the size of a fist are $3, larger items $5. The dresses cost $20.

We are at the enormous Long Beach Veterans Memorial Stadium. On a Sunday morning, the lines are quite long. For the best luck, you have to arrive early.

Fairfax and Melrose

At the intersection of Fairfax and Melrose Avenues in Hollywood lies a big parking lot that is transformed into a great flea market with decent prices every Sunday. Here's a lady wearing a flowered hat, a veil, and fancy gloves. She's selling everything from an old copper faucet decorated with cherubs to a necklace with a magical-looking pearl. The next booth over sells ceramics from the '70s.

The last stop is the Santa Monica Airport Outdoor Antique and Collectible Market. It's a bit exciting to drive right next to the landing strip. Here are Peruvian rugs crammed together with Hollywood steel-tube furniture that shines and glimmers, reflecting the California sun. Keep an eye out for these special items at the flea markets.

FLEA MARKET CHECKLIST

1. Wooden crates
2. Old windows
3. Sculptures
4. Disco balls
5. Tassels
6. Crystals
7. Wooden face masks
8. Embroidered fabric
9. Oil paintings, preferably portraits
10. Dream catchers
11. Skateboards and surfboards

Jungle Décor

There are many beaches in Los Angeles, and the desert is close by, but equally close is an abundance of full-blown greenery. The greenery outside is often reflected inside in this city. If you live in a cooler climate, then focus on greenery indoors by putting plants in unexpected places, such as a dresser drawer.

GET THE LOOK

1. Choose a plant that doesn't require a lot of water, such as a succulent.

2. Use something watertight, such as a plastic bag, to plant in. Cover the bottom with expanded clay pellets and fill up with soil.

3. Place the soil bag in the drawer.

4. Plant your plant in the bag.

Greenhouse Oasis

Dark green paint gives depth and can enhance the jungle feel. But don't take it too far—just a few green accents or a background wall is enough. With small shelves you can create a little greenhouse in the window.

GET THE LOOK

1. Cut shelves and purchase brackets based on your window measurements.

2. Paint the shelves, brackets, and window frame in the same dark green as your wall.

3. Screw the brackets, evenly spaced, to the window frame. Remember to make enough space—at least 20 in/51 cm—between shelves for pots and vases.

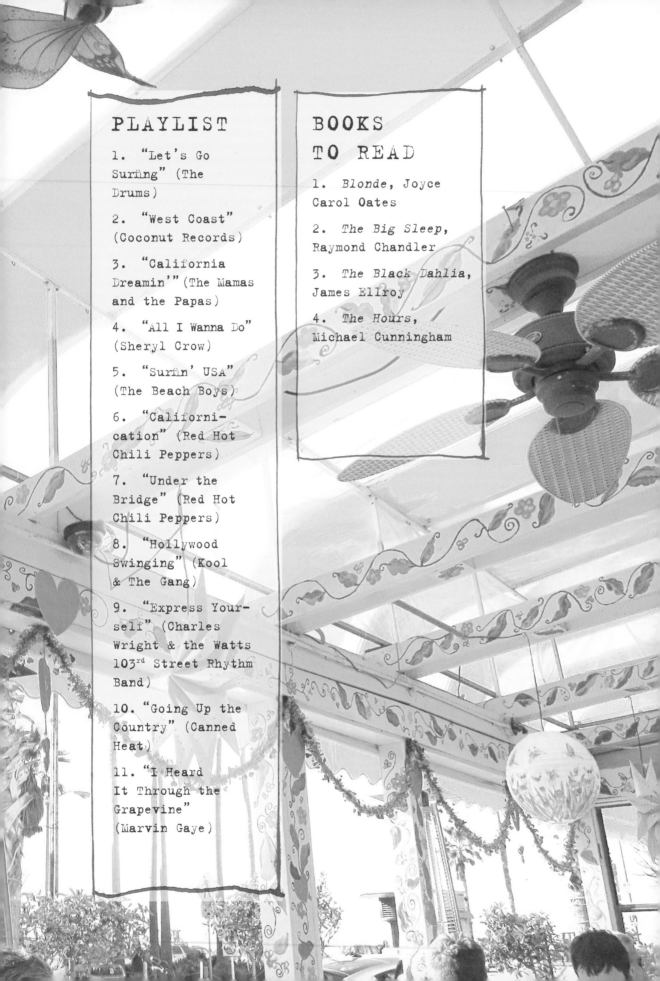

PLAYLIST

1. "Let's Go Surfing" (The Drums)

2. "West Coast" (Coconut Records)

3. "California Dreamin'" (The Mamas and the Papas)

4. "All I Wanna Do" (Sheryl Crow)

5. "Surfin' USA" (The Beach Boys)

6. "Californi-cation" (Red Hot Chili Peppers)

7. "Under the Bridge" (Red Hot Chili Peppers)

8. "Hollywood Swinging" (Kool & The Gang)

9. "Express Your-self" (Charles Wright & the Watts 103rd Street Rhythm Band)

10. "Going Up the Country" (Canned Heat)

11. "I Heard It Through the Grapevine" (Marvin Gaye)

BOOKS TO READ

1. *Blonde*, Joyce Carol Oates

2. *The Big Sleep*, Raymond Chandler

3. *The Black Dahlia*, James Ellroy

4. *The Hours*, Michael Cunningham

"Dreams are
necessary to life."

Anaïs Nin

The Hippie Bed

4 steps to a hippie-style bedroom

✔ Fashion a canopy by using a curtain with rod pockets in preferably a light, slightly transparent fabric. Spread out the curtain and attach it to a curtain rod on the wall (or over the window if possible). Pull a string or rope through the other end of the fabric, cinch the fabric together, and tie it to a hook hanging from the ceiling.

✔ Find an unusual statement piece to finish off the canopy, like the crocheted lampshade pictured on the right.

✔ If your bed is against a wall, you can make a decorative "head-board" from fabric or a painting placed on the wall behind the bed. Try green ocean colors with hints of beach yellow.

✔ Cover the bed with a comforter in Pacific Ocean blue that gives depth and ties in with the headboard. Mix pillows of different styles: knitted with yarn fringes and glittery with sequins.

tip

A brown ceiling gives an unexpected calm to the room.

Fez 1495R-WN

Installations

Use a neglected corner for an art installation the Angeleno way.
Put your collage near a window and watch it gleam in the sunlight.

On the ceiling: Hang a woven basket for a playful look. You
can also try a lamp or hanging flowerpot at the perfect height
between the paintings.

On the wall: Pick out your favorite pictures. Portraits of unknown
(or known) people can eventually turn into good friends.

On the floor: Evoke the ever-present Pacific Ocean with some
cork floats found on the beach. Mix them with some paintings
overlapped and placed randomly. Consider putting one painting
with its back facing out to create curiosity. Pots with tall green
plants combined with the plant hanging on the wall tie the room
together.

The Color Palette

The palette in Los Angeles can be everything from peaceful and calm to bright and colorful. Many homes feature hues of the desert mixed with richer jungle tones, often with a base of brown.

Sand

Camel

Off-white

Cream

Jungle green

Jade green

Pacific Ocean blue

Brown

Crimson red

Dream Catcher

The dream catcher is believed to have originated with the Ojibwe tribe in North America. The spiderweb interior is said to catch bad dreams and only let the best ones slip through the hole in the middle.

GET THE LOOK

1. Twist together thin, bendable twigs to make a ring. Tie the twigs with twine. One ring is enough, but you can make more if you want. If desired, wrap thin strips of leather around the ring.

2. Wrap string across the ring to form a web, taking care to leave a hole open in the center. Alternatively, you can attach an old crocheted cloth with glue or a coarse mesh with a hole in the middle.

3. Embellish the bottom of your dream catcher by stringing beads on thread or strips of leather. Finish off the ends with a feather. Tie these elements to the bottom, allowing enough space for each strand to move freely. Tie another piece of thread or leather to the top of the dream catcher and make a loop.

4. Hang your dream catcher over the bed. If you made several of them, group them as a central piece in your room.

Angelenos incorporate elements from the city's cultural mix into their homes. With immigrants from 140 countries living in this dense city, there's no ethnic majority, and the cultural landscape shows it. From Little Tokyo to Little Central America, small districts are scattered around L.A., and the culture of the city reflects the vibrant mix of ethnicities. Other legacies are also visible, like the California surf and hippie style. This is reflected in the décor, from Japanese wooden dolls on display, African masks hung on walls, wooden peace symbols cluttered on shelves, and surfboards casually leaning against walls.

Still Life à la L.A.

Home Style by City

MOVIES
TO WATCH

1. *Short Cuts*,
Robert Altman

2. *The Kids Are
All Right*, Lisa
Cholodenko

3. *Sunset Boulevard*,
Billy Wilder

4. *Pulp Fiction*,
Quentin Tarantino

5. *The Artist*,
Michel Hazanavicius

Good-bye,
L.A.

Copenhagen

Copenhagen's soul is stylish
and easygoing. In the Copenhagen
apartment, gray-painted wood
floors creak, and drafty windows
cause candles to flicker. The classic
1950s sofa is ready for Danish
coziness, a perfect setting for cups
of coffee in ornate blue mugs from
Royal Copenhagen.

Facades are in pastel and ocher.
Next to the front doors grow
hollyhocks, and through an open
window you can hear small talk
and Danish songs.

The secret:
A chic foundation with room
for the ornate.

Copenhagen's Mood

Where does that mix of the cosmopolitan and small-town ambience come from? There's the cool Nordic light, the breeze of Paris boulevards, and at the same time a bit of country idyll. And then there are the fairy-tale castles in the middle of the city: Amalienborg, the rococo palace where the royal family lives in winter, and Rosenborg, a castle in renaissance style in the middle of Kongens Have.

Character

Right next to the pedestrian street Strøget and the cobblestone squares are narrow, crooked alleyways. That's where you find the small, simple apartments, in houses where until recently you would meet your neighbors in their bathrobes on the way down to the shared shower in the basement. (Maybe that's one of the reasons for the almost family-like atmosphere of Copenhagen.) The backyards shimmer in tones of gold from the ocher-painted buildings with walls half covered in ivy.

Cultural Heritage

With its carousels and cotton candy, Tivoli, the amusement park in the center of Copenhagen, has been spreading joy since 1843. But it is the statue of the Little Mermaid that is the signature of the city—a lovely homage to Hans Christian Andersen's wistfully sad story about the youngest daughter of the king of the sea who falls in love with a human prince. And let's not forget the light in the works of the Skagen painters and the modern furniture designers' sense of style, part of the Copenhagen heritage.

3 steps for getting in the Danish mood

- ✔ Listen to Carl Nielsen's piece for flute and harp, "Tågen letter."
- ✔ Get inspired by Marie Krøyer's art and let the Nordic lightness in.
- ✔ Mix the darkness of Danish movies with Nordic elegance, exemplified by supermodel and icon Helena Christensen.

tip

The Scandinavian light can be glorious, but Copenhagen lacks light a good portion of the year, so many bring light sources into their homes. In one room you might find a ceiling lamp, a floor lamp, a wall lamp, and candles on the table.

Nordic Style

Your way to a typical Copenhagen room

What do Copenhageners surround themselves with? Something homemade, something classic, and something that surprises and stands out.

At the center of the Copenhagen room is almost always an inherited design classic from the mid-1900s. Such treasures might be from one of the great designers: Mogensen, Jacobsen, Hansen, or Juhl, just to name a few.

But don't feel you have to be loyal to any specific designer. Any piece of teak furniture is a good start for your Scandinavian room.

Next you must soften the stylish, straight lines of the '50s and '60s with some paint and a bit of an artisan touch.

- ✔ Homemade quilted pillows and a patchwork in pastels.
- ✔ Woven blankets with expressive patterns.
- ✔ Something well worn, like a leather armchair with soft, rounded edges.
- ✔ Paintings, graphic art, and embroidery on the wall.

Make It a Bit Disordered

Create a lively wall by hanging pictures ever so asymmetrically. How does one do that without making the arrangement too orderly or too disorganized? The Copenhagen secret is to make it sloppy in a perfect way:

1. Measure where you want your pictures as you would do it conventionally. Use a level, a measuring tape, and a pencil. Try to keep your art aligned at the top. Hammer in the nails and hang the pictures.

2. Now, take everything down. Mix up the pictures randomly and hang them to get a completely different expression. Try it a few times so they don't overlap or look too messy, and feel free to move a nail down slightly so that your wall reflects the perfect level of disarray.

Unexpected Details

It's now that the Copenhagen woman starts to stray. She's not seeking a perfectly polished home, but rather, adds some unexpected elements. Everything from pairing a fishbone wood floor and a grand chandelier with a large quilt à la the 1970s on the wall and a Moroccan Bedouin tent in the living room.

It is still important to keep a cool and typically Nordic base and not stray too far. The unexpected must remain as details. If you add too many, they overwhelm the space and miss the point.

Design Classics

The Y-chair,
Hans J. Wegner

The PH-lamp,
Poul Henningsen

The Ant Chair,
Arne Jacobsen

The Safari Chair,
Kaare Klint

Tremmesofa (page 132),
Børge Mogensen

Monkey (page 140),
Kay Bojesen

Prince Chair,
Louise Campbell

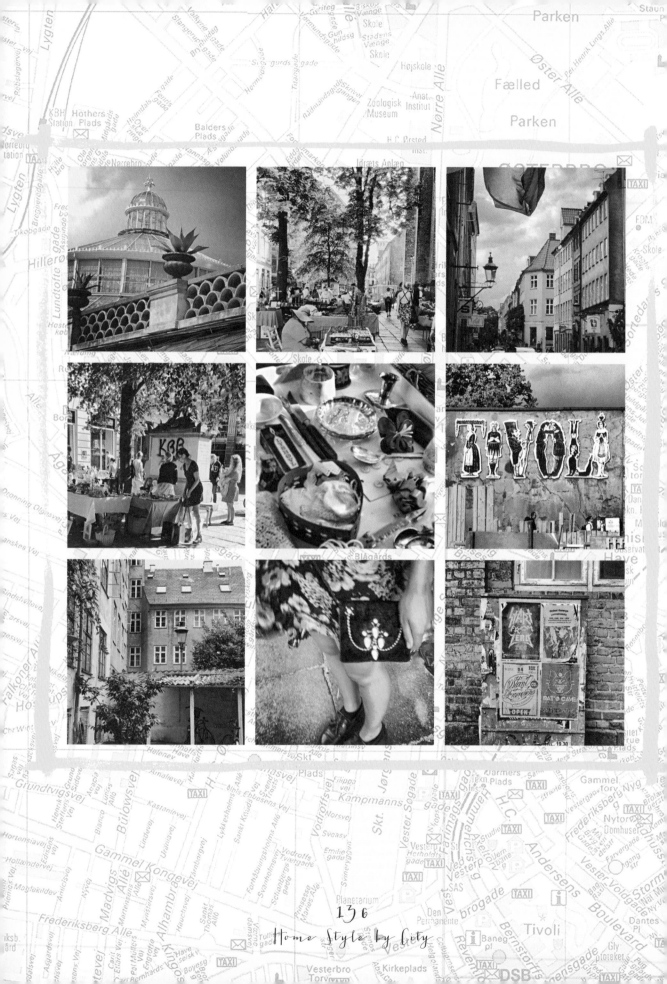

Copenhagen Flea Markets

On Saturdays and Sundays, and sometimes on a midweek afternoon, all the antiques shops on Ravnsborggade are open. The street—filled with Danish porcelain, Musselmalet patterned soup bowls, and teapots—is located in Nørrebro, on the other side of Søerne, the Lakes. Some Sundays there is also a flea market.

Picnic

From Nørrebro you can keep walking to Assistens Cemetery, where Danish celebrities like the philosopher Søren Kierkegaard and the furniture designer Finn Juhl are buried. If you're lucky, you'll find a flea market along the yellow wall. If not, it's still worth the walk; bring a coffee and sit down on the lawn among the tombstones and other picnicking Copenhageners.

Delicate Things

The finest flea market is located under the big leafy trees at Trinitatis Kirke (Trinity Church) along Købmagergade, right by Rundetårn. It's particularly beautiful on a summer day when the green leaves glisten. Here, many people have set up tables with Copenhagen specialties. There are decanters, chandelier prisms, quilts, and beautiful scarves. A woman in a hat sells amber necklaces, and another in a hat has fallen asleep in the sun. As you wander the flea markets, look to this list to bring Copenhagen home with you.

FLEA MARKET CHECKLIST

1. Royal Copenhagen porcelain
2. Teak furniture
3. Stuffed animals
4. Plates
5. Chandeliers
6. Wood drawers, preferably from a dresser
7. A quilt, or fabric to make one
8. Embroidered pictures
9. Lamps
10. Vases
11. Wallpaper
12. Cutting boards

The Danish Kitchen

Using cotton candy pink is one of the Copenhagen tricks to liven up a tiny kitchen where there is no room to sit. Another simple trick is to open up the wall and make a window or a bar counter between the rooms. There you can relax and have a quick bite, help out by peeling or chopping, or just sit and socialize.

tips

For displaying and storing:

- A round marble tray with a hole in the center: Wind a string between the outside edge and the hole all the way around the tray. It's a simple and smart way to display notes and mementos.

- A cork trivet: perfect for attaching little notes with thumb tacks.

Upgrade old drawers from a dresser to make utilitarian and unexpected kitchen shelves.

GET THE LOOK

1. Use at least three drawers and place them approximately 20 in/51 cm apart so that the top also serves as a shelf.

2. Drill holes and screw each shelf to the wall.

Drawer
Shelf

The Copenhagen dining room radiates coziness or *hygge*—and is at the same time decorated with exciting details and combinations that arouse curiosity.

Dining Room Details

3 steps to a dining room with Danish hygge

✔ Now it's time to start mixing styles. Think about Danish harmonies and bringing out that Scandinavian personality. Mix classic heirlooms with the modern.

✔ Enjoy the Nordic tradition of socializing at home. Look for very comfortable chairs, preferably with frames and armrests, so that they invite deep, long discussions. You also need a large table—with lots of room, even for people who just happen to stop by. Facing the table might be a system of shelves holding a lively display of objects that stimulates conversation: encyclopedias, old books, pens, paper.

✔ To compensate for the lack of light, select an assortment of light fixtures. With three different lamps that have the same basic structure, you get an exciting and varied impression with nice lighting over the long table.

tips

This colorful mix of furniture and décor requires a calm background. A light wood floor and a subtle purple color on the walls rein in and relax the atmosphere. A vanilla-yellow wall gives a milder impression, ocher yellow is more intense, and blue hues lend a calm and cool feel.

Bookcase Blues

The fancier Copenhagen apartment is equipped with an old-fashioned ornamental masonry heater. Most homes don't have this fine detail, so it's best to focus on another statement piece in the room, such as a bookcase with the books sorted by color. Experiment with the right layout for your books, and place some colorful objects, like a collection of green vases, atop the shelf.

"To live is not enough. . . .One must also have sunshine, freedom, and a little flower."

Hans Christian Andersen, 1805–1875

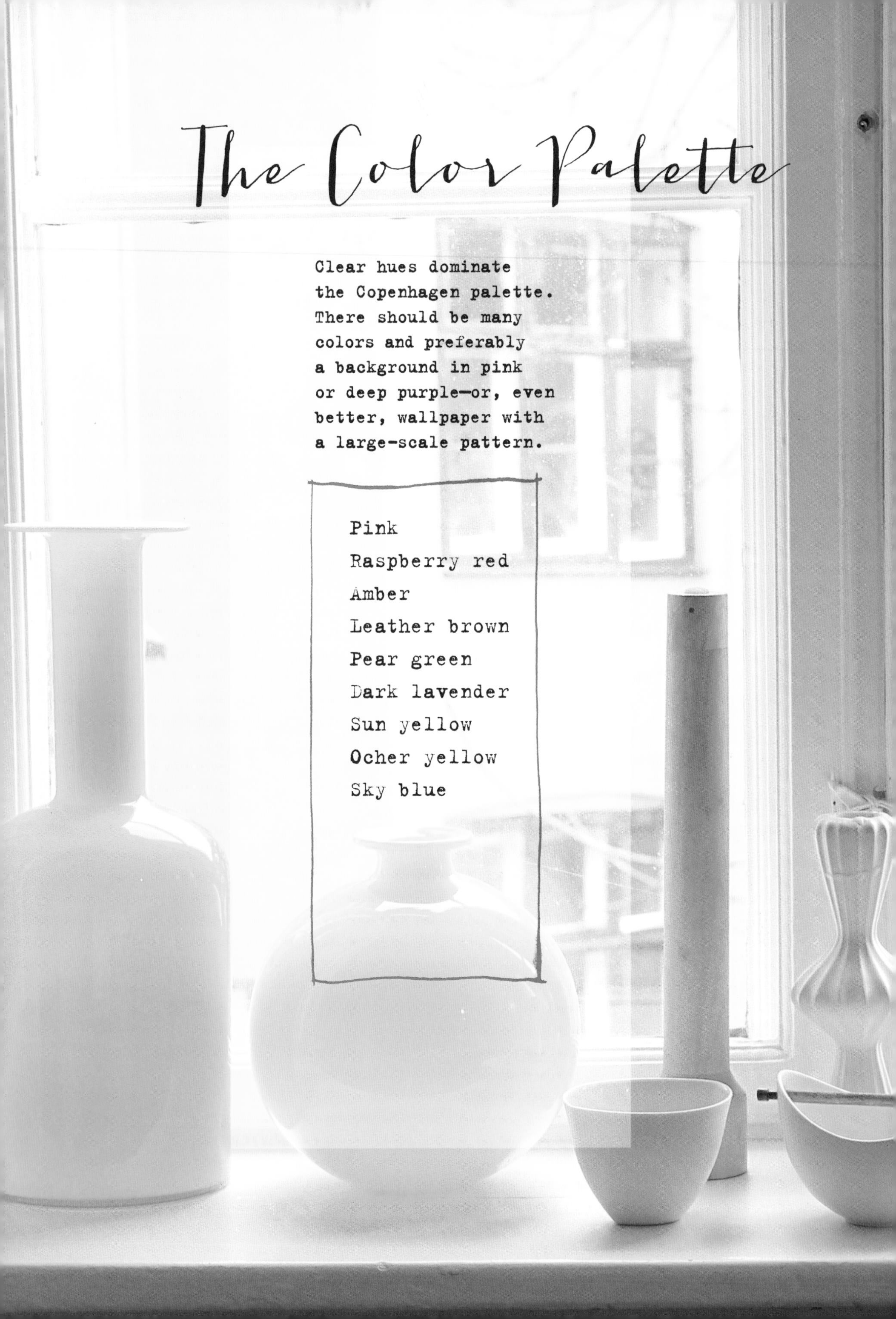

The Color Palette

Clear hues dominate
the Copenhagen palette.
There should be many
colors and preferably
a background in pink
or deep purple—or, even
better, wallpaper with
a large-scale pattern.

Pink

Raspberry red

Amber

Leather brown

Pear green

Dark lavender

Sun yellow

Ocher yellow

Sky blue

147
Copenhagen

The Copenhagen still life is built on themes and small collections. Search for an assortment of objects of the same type—stuffed animals in one place, vases in another, and a dozen china plates on the wall.

The Copenhagen Collection

plate collection

sticker collection

Wall of Plates

152

Bookcase Light

Because we are in Copenhagen, where the sun sets early, we must focus on finding the perfectly stylish light.

GET THE LOOK

1. Figure out where in the bookcase the lighting would be best.

2. Attach a small hook on which to hang the lamp.

3. Drill a hole in the side of the bookcase.

4. Pull the cord through the hook and the hole.

5. Connect the plug and turn on the light.

Wallpaper
Mix and Match

Mix and match patterns and vintage wallpaper on everything from walls to mirror frames for an authentic Copenhagen look. Use any leftover scraps to decorate other objects around the home.

GET THE LOOK

1. Measure what you want to decorate—shelf, mirror, drawer, or something else. Cut the wallpaper according to the measurements.

2. For a small surface, use wood glue to attach the wallpaper pieces to your item.

3. Smooth out the wallpaper with a sponge to remove any bubbles. Let dry.

BOOKS TO READ

1. *Smilla's Sense of Snow*, Peter Høeg

2. *The Crown Princess*, Hanne-Vibeke Holst

3. *The Exception*, Christian Jungersen

4. *Let Us*, collection of poetry, Lone Hørslev

5. *Kick Me in the Traditions*, Leif Panduro

MOVIES AND TV SHOWS TO WATCH

1. *The One and Only*, Susanne Bier

2. *Shake It All About*, Hella Joof

3. *Borgen* (TV series), Adam Price

4. *The Celebration*, Thomas Vinterberg

5. *A Royal Affair*, Nikolaj Arcel

PLAYLIST

1. "Tågen letter" (Carl Nielsen, piece for flute and harp)

2. "Riverside" (Agnes Obel)

3. "Wonderful Copenhagen" (Danny Kaye)

4. "Let Your Fingers Do the Walking" (Sort Sol)

5. "Valby bakke" (Peter Sommer)

6. "Christiania kampsang" (Osiris)

7. "Jeg snakker med mig selv" (Gitte Hænning)

8. "Love in a Trashcan" (The Raveonettes)

Photo Credits

All photos by Ida Magntorn, except pages 4, 5, 114, 126, 127 by Mira Magntorn.

FEATURED HOMES

Paris

Anna Malmberg,
www.annamalmbergphoto
.com, pages 10, 13, 18–21,
26–27, 30, 32, 33 top right, 35

Lovisa Burfitt Rigby,
www.lovisaburfitt.com,
pages 22–23, 25

Katrin Jakobsen,
pages 16–17

Ulf Clervall,
background photo on cover page
and page 7

Céline Vitcoq,
page 33 left and bottom right

London

Emily Chalmers,
www.emilychalmers.com,
www.caravanstyle.com,
pages 42, 45, 50–51, 55, 62 top
and right, 63, 66–67

Emily Henson,
www.emilyhensonstudio.com,
pages 59, 62 left

Lou Rota,
www.lourota.com,
pages 1, 48, 52–53, 56–57

Gregory Watson,
pages 49, 54, 60–61, 62 bottom

Bobby Petersen,
www.bobbypetersen.com,
pages 38, 58

New York

Johanna Burke,
www.burkeandpryde.com,
back cover, pages 72–75, 86–87,
100

Johanna Methusalemsdottir,
www.kriajewelry.com,
pages 80–81, 84–85

Simon Howell and
Jessica Barensfeld,
www.lynnandlawrence.com,
www.jessicabarensfeld.com,
pages 76–77, 98–99

Digby & Iona,
www.digbyandiona.com,
pages 88–89, 96–97

Ariele Alasko,
www.arielealasko.com,
pages 82–83

Julia Small,
www.smallstudio.blogspot.com,
pages 94–95

Kelli Anderson,
page 93

Los Angeles

Faith Blakeney,
www.callmefaith.com,
pages 100–101, 104–105, 107,
113, 115

Justina Blakeney,
www.blog.justinablakeney.com,
pages 116–117, 124 bottom

Tracy Wilkinson,
www.tracywilkinson.net,
pages 118–119, 121–123,
125 right

Derek James, Kristin Korven,
www.fromlookoutmountain
.com, pages 112, 124

Copenhagen

Mette Helena Rasmussen,
www.mettehelena.dk,
www.retrovilla.dk,
pages 132, 140 right and bottom
left, 141–142, 155

Lisa Grue,
www.underwerket.blogspot.com,
pages 128, 134–135, 140 top
right, 146–147, 150, 152–153

Kristine Meyer,
www.meyerlavigne.dk,
pages 138–139, 144–145, 148 top
and bottom, 157

Mette Hartvig Johnsson,
pages 148 right and left, 151, 154

Acknowledgments

Thank you to everyone who helped me create this book:

Mira Magntorn, who was my assistant during my travels and flea market visits, and who helped me with the text, photos, concept, and design.

Erik and Måns Magntorn, our trustworthy companions.

Photographer Tine Guth Linse and photographer Jenny Leyman.

Henrik Skogh, Mia Krokstäde, Hanna Welin.

Julia Bristulf, who designed the frame.

The book club: Karin Nykvist, Hélène Mönnich Börjeson, Malin Sandström, Victoria Söderberg, for the book and movie discussions that filled up my lists. And Kattis Brundenius.

Liza Larsson-Alvarez, Lisa Karindotter Pålsson, Karin Fremer.

Clara Bolmsjö, Andrea de la Barre de Nanteuil.

Petra Ward, Ebba Östberg, Gabriella Sahlin, Susanna Höijer at Norstedts Agency, and Cecilia Ljungström.

Stefan Ohlsson/Le Nord.

And, of course, all of you from the previous pages, you who opened your homes to me, told me your stories, and let me take pictures. Thank you!

About the Author

Ida Magntorn is a writer and photographer with a focus on interior design. In addition to writing two other books, Ida has been editor-in-chief of the *Sydsvenskan* home and living section as well as the antique and flea market pages of various magazines. She is also a free-lance reporter and a blogger for *Elle Decoration*.

Photo by Jenny Leyman

First published in the United States of America in
2014 by Chronicle Books LLC.

First published in Sweden in 2013 by Norstedts as Urban Vintage.

Library of Congress Cataloging-in-Publication
Data available.

ISBN: 978-1-4521-3717-9

Manufactured in China

Design, photography, and illustration:
Ida Magntorn
Production: Cecilia Ljungstrom
Prepress: Fälth & Hässler

City map of New York, pages 78–79: Map provided
courtesy of Esri. Data for the map provided courtesy
of Esri, DeLorme, NAVTEQ, increment P Corp.,
EPA, USGS, and NPS.

10 9 8 7 6 5 4 3

Chronicle Books LLC
680 Second Street
San Francisco, California 94107
www.chroniclebooks.com

Fez 1495R-WN